POEMS FROM WALDEN

POEMS FROM WALDEN
GORDON E. MCNEER

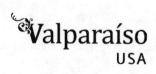

Valparaíso
USA

Number 38 in the Valparaíso Poetry Collection

Cover Design: Chari Nogales

First Edition in USA: Febraury 2021

© For the poems: Gordon E. McNeer

© Valparaíso Editions USA, LLC
POB 1729. Clayton, GA 30525 USA
www.valparaisoeditions.us

ISBN: 978-1-951370-10-7

Printed in the United States of America

Valparaíso USA, POB 1729, Clayton, GA 30525 USA

POEMS FROM WALDEN

Dedicated to the poets
of the Uncertainty Group

ELIOT

Time future and time past
are the flotsam
of this foundering soul
that finds itself adrift
in the darkest night of nights.

I can write the word *nightingale*
and a birdsong erupts in a thicket.
The song has a beginning and an end,
a future and a past and its moment,
but what does its sweet song mean?

To read Eliot is to drink in
the river of our existence:
we flicker, fade and flow downstream...
a river raging through a field of dreams.

To read Eliot is to learn
that the forest exists
without the trees,
and that the trees exist
without the forest.

To read Eliot is to know
that the lighthouse turns
to illuminate your soul,
that the lighthouse turns

and leaves you in the throes
of a darkness too dark to know.

What good is your poetry
if its past and its future
will be lost in a time that is not time
if its meaning is meaning
bereft of meaning.

What good is your poetry
if it leaves you
helpless like a rich man's child.

WOUND

A wound is God's mouth
questioning the universe.
God's eyes
staring back at us.
It is a hunger for
our carbon copy among the stars.

A wound is the Big Bang
inside of us searching
for peace and tranquility
in the face of our own violence
the savage nature
of our creation.

A wound is our fear of self
a black hole beyond reason
the broken pieces
of the puzzle
that is our salvation.

ALL I REALLY WANT TO DO

For Vicente Aleixandre

To grow old
to cross a bridge
and let the waters down below
stir the child and set the stone.

To feel the evening
shadows come to rest
upon our shoulders
-the cold the dread-
broken blood and bones
of those gone on ahead.

To listen to the voice
that bids us stay a while.
To listen to the soul
that fears the darkness
vast and wide and cries
out in pain but not surrender.

To see and feel these moments
—to remember them—
and to be remembered.

AMERICAN PIE

The day the music died
I was driving down a road
alongside a railroad track
from Lake Alfred to Auburndale.
The day the music died
Don McLean was singing
American Pie on the radio.
There were oranges in the air
and there was sunlight.
There was a young man
who had no idea
that all things must die,
including the young man.
The day the music died
he was awake, he was alive,
and yet he could feel
the words in the song:
the Joker, the Devil,
the marching band,
and he knew that something
was coming to an end,
irrevocably, unconditionally,
worthy of any Greek tragedy.

GOD AND THE DEVIL

God and the Devil
talking in the schoolyard:
talking about hatred
talking about love.
The child in the darkness
stands by and listens,
to God and the Devil
talking about hatred
talking about love.

The moon keeps on rising,
the sun keeps on setting
the shadows grow longer
and get down on their knees.
The snake's in the garden
with an eye to the maiden
as an apple keeps falling
from a very old tree.

The child in the schoolyard
has two angels to guide him
they sit on his shoulders
and do as they please.
One whispers softly
a breeze from the hilltops.
The other moans gently
a lament by the sea.

The child in the schoolyard
hears the angels that guide him,
sees the snake in the garden,
hears the owl in the tree,
sees the maiden's long tresses
while the apple keeps falling,
and God and the Devil
keep talking, keep talking
about love, about hatred
in strange harmony.

ANNIE

I remember the long straight legs
—or were they short-
with your back to me
dressed only in a thong
and framed in a doorway by Dalí,
a camera hanging from each hand.
You were perfection: pigtails,
Indian blood that seethed
beneath a portrait by Ingres.
But then you started drinking,
smoking weed, shooting dope.
When you fell down the stairs
and broke your back
and your spirit broke
the last thing on your mind
was Bob Dylan.

FULCRUM

In the picture you are seeking balance.
It is not life or death,
you are in a shop in Las Vegas
and not on the western rim
of the Grand Canyon
with that two-thousand-mile-deep crack
between your legs and the wind
pushing you ever so gently toward the precipice...
And yet this is a serious moment in your life,
you are on the brink of a milestone:
the clock yields to the master's hand
in the *Persistence of Memory,*
and yet it is still a clock
and continues to record conscious time,
as fair from fair declines.

IMAGINE

I was laying on the couch
and all of a sudden
they were playing the Beatles
over and over and over.
It made no sense
until I learned of your death.
Not long before that I had heard you say:
Life begins at forty.
You were forty and you were gunned down
on December 8th, one day after Pearl Harbor Day.

Forty years later it's your birthday
and I try to made sense
of the second half of a life that doesn't exist.
And I think back on that morning climbing up the fence
with you and Zimmy on Miracle Mile
watching the President go by, and you said:
One thing you can't hide is when you're crippled inside.

IVAN'S DREAM

As in Ivan's dream
in the *Brothers Karamazov*
when the Devil came to visit
he was a business man with a cold.
In my dream at 30,000 feet
the Angel that sat down beside me
was a business man from the Bronx,
and a very unpleasant individual.
Later on, the Angel spoke to me,
and told me I would surely die,
but that somehow
everything was going to be alright.
And I felt relief, I felt comforted
by the gentle touch on my shoulder,
and I fell into a profound sleep.

JESUS AND THE NOBEL PRIZE

If Jesus were alive
would he get
the Nobel Prize
for Peace on Earth
and Good Will to Man
or would they hand it
to his Second in Command,
the Prince of Darkness,
the Devil?

One condition of the prize
is that to receive it
you must be alive:
you must do more
than roll the stone away
to the astonishment
of family and friends alike.
You must do more than
turn water to wine,
stones to bread,
and bring back the dead to life.
Levitation is not required.
You must be somebody
internationally admired.

RENAISSANCE

In this painting,
a dream by Botticelli,
there is an angel
holding a bouquet
of pale pink roses,
who reminds him
as he sleeps fitfully
of yet another vision,
that he will paint some day:
the *Birth of Venus*.

You could be that angel
looking down from the doorway
of any Gothic cathedral,
watching over the faithful
as they come in to pray
with their heads bowed
—not for you—
but for their own salvation,
comforted by seeing you
carved in stone triumphant
and watching over them.

I look at you and hear you say
as we lie together in our sleep:
some poems need a picture
to create them. While others
lead you far away to dream.

SANDRO

For T.S. Eliot

It took you nine full years
to paint your masterpiece.
Nine full years observing
Simonetta Vespucci
as the two of you redefined
what is beautiful
in the streets of Florence
and birds and flowers
and other avatars
went mad at the sight of her
and you made the invisible
become visible for a moment
as it sang her praise in the air.

And when you died,
according to your wishes,
nothing changed in your city
for five hundred years.
No one could breathe the vapors
that lingered in her breast.
No one could kneel down
to worship the memory
 of her footsteps pressed deep
within the cobblestones.
You were buried at her feet
just out of reach of their fragrance

as the ineffable became effable
for a moment, only to fade away once again.

FERLINGHETTI

It was a face that darkness could kill in an instant.
LAWRENCE FERLINGHETTI

Yours is a face too fragile
for the light of day
only that moment
when the flowers
begin to tremble
in anticipation
only that moment
when the birds
seek shelter
in the twilight haze
only that moment
when the moon
rises up in the blood
of a sun that must die
will do you justice.

And you ask why
poets paint
and sculptors sculpt
and lovers languish
before a face that darkness
could kill in an instant?
Consider when Paris first laid eyes on Helen
and started a war.
Consider when Mary Magdalene
sat with Christ at the Last Supper.

Consider the Italian Renaissance
when men carved their dreams in stone
for all to see.
My only answer is Botticelli.
Botticelli, Botticelli.

VIRUS

My friends say
you're a poet
write about the virus,
as if the virus
was worth writing about.

The indifference
of God's plan
has finally become
obvious to all of us.

There is no
Mother Nature
and there is no
Father Time

God is a concept
by which we measure
our pain
as John goes down
in front of the Dakota.

Today, Cervantes
was born.
Today, Artemisa and Gordon
were married
in a place called Lake Alfred.

They had lives to live,
promises to keep.
And all the while,
their cancers were
lying in ambush
as sure as God
makes green apples.

YOU SAY YOU WANT A REVOLUTION

To John, Che and Fidel

Burn baby burn.
It doesn't matter
If it's Torquemada
or Donald Trump.
Joan of Arc
or Patty Smith.
Jesus giving a peck
on the cheek
of the Grand Inquisitor
in Ivan's dream.

It doesn't matter if its 1968
or last night on CNBC,
Fox News or the WSJ.
It doesn't matter
if it's our inner cities
or the Redwoods in California:
we are all combustible,
we are all on fire
in our own way,
in our own self-righteousness.
Looters dance in the cities,
outrage stalks the land.
The good folk
stay close to their bibles and guns.
We want change
but in our own image.

It's only rock 'n roll,
grunge or hip hop,
but we like it.
Wait for Face Book,
Instagram or TikTok
to tell you who you are,
to nail you to your car.
22 November 1963.
Bob Dylan mourns
A Murder Most Foul.
The greatest magic trick of all
performed before a live audience.

And that's when the lies began:
The Warren Report, Viet Nam,
Watergate, the 27 Club,
HIV, let's kill those deviants.
The Twin Towers, New York City in flames,
Weapons of Mass Destruction,
endless war, Goya, Goya, Goya
SARS, MERS, COVID: plague plain and simple.
Launch the infected bodies over the walls.
Yellow matter custard
dripping from a dead dog's eye.
Send the infected tourists here first class.
Show them fire, burn baby burn.
Show them love, but give them hate.
Show them compassion, but strike a match,
girl, start anew: *it's all over now, baby blue.*

18 AUGUST

For all of you

Federico Federico Federico
your death is a wound
that will never heal.
There is an olive tree
that remembers your blood
and sand that cradles your remains,
but nowhere is there a shadow
that bears your name
because you are gone forever,
and I can still hear your words
as they call out from your grave:

Walk me down by the olive trees
and murder me there:
someday they will look for me,
but they will find only the scent
of wildcat and thistles and honeysuckle.

Walk me down along the riverbanks
and murder me there,
where young girls have thighs like the trout
that swim in the icy green waters
and their lovers are gypsies and thieves.

Walk me through the streets of my Granada
and murder me there,

where the moon wears lace dresses
that froth up over the broken wine glasses of dawn.

Yes, murder me again and again and again,
among the olive trees,
where a guitar can be heard but not seen
weeping and crying out for love,
and tuberoses stretch their necks like swans
swimming in a memory of origin and ashes.

Murder me there, in the flower of my youth,
because only the moon suspects the truth...

INSISTENCE

For Fernando Valverde

Evil exists:
it is palpable
in the breath
of a newborn child
that returns
to the womb every night.

This time it will be different.
She forces a smile
and then forgets
your name your face your eyes
the reason why
you hide inside the lives
of the Cheshire cat.

Evil exists:
you can feel it grow
like the hair
on the back of your neck
like the saliva
that dries in your mouth
and turns your spit
into prayers,
into everything
you've ever feared.

I love you
will never be enough:
there is only you,
no god to pull you through.
The Mad Hatter
 hands you an egg
and says scramble me,
and so you do,
but the pain
becomes more intense,
it crackles all over your skin
like shingles, like leprosy,
like HIV, like Hepatitis C.

Evil exists:
you turn the lights out
but they stay on in your mind.
It is a cloak you wear day and night.
There is no name for it
so you call it the insistence of harm.
Others call it karma, fate, destiny.
It is the nameless creature
that Kafka saw in the mirror,
The horror visited on Kurtz
in the Heart of Darkness.
The force that drove the nails
 into the body of Christ.

There is no name for it,
but it exists, insists, persists…
Evil exists.

CHIAROSCURO

When Kafka looked in the mirror
it wasn't a bug that he saw.
It was the paint that Picasso
mixed to draw *Les Demoiselles*.
It was what was on the end of the fork
in Burroughs's *Naked Lunch*.
Ferlinghetti's *face that darkness*
could kill an instant.
The horror that Kurtz
could taste in the back of his throat.
Cervantes' six teeth.
The gaping hole in the back
of the Great White Whale.

Every morning I get up
to paint myself
into the rising sun,
but the darkness hangs on longer,
like a shadow that whispers Caravaggio.

GALÁN

Everything you do will be forgotten.
The river has run its course
and the stones are left to sleep in its depths.
The stones you left unturned
will be left unturned,
only to be left unturned again.
There is a rhythm that escapes us:
it is my life it is your life it is our life.

I could say I am Bob Dylan
writing about the *Insistence of Harm,*
but instead I write your names:
palimpsest, alias, zimmy.
You who will never read these lines,
dig into my skin and you will find
the seeds of our death.
Plant them and watch the sun rise
in Alaska in Mexico in Lake Alfred.

I could say I am Bob Dylan
placing pennies on the eyes of the Jesuit priests,
they were not the only ones,
you say, *there were so many more,*
but instead I feel your hand inside my hand,
and I grow silent listening, waiting
for the master's voice
to plant seeds in the mind of the Pope:
I don't care if they kill me, this story must be told

you said one day at lunch.
Plant the seeds and watch them grow
in San Salvador in the Vatican in Madrid in New York.

I could say you are Bob Dylan
writing your last song in the graveyards of the living
about the murders of so many in the minds of so few,
about the men with their hammers all bleeding
about a white man who walks a black dog
about the masters of war and the cars that they drive
about the Jesuit priests that hang from the windows
all along the watchtowers and into our lives.

SURPRISE

To Federico

You were flopping around like a fish
in the market place.
Nobody knew who you were.
There was a bullet hole
where your right eye was supposed to be
and lots of blood.
I kept telling you that you would be alright.
Later, the pimps drove by to show the other girls
what happens when they get out of line.
Later still — thirty years went by — I realize
I don't remember the pop from the 25
or the police who surely came
to take your lifeless body off of mine.
You were dead in my eyes
and nobody knew who you were.

WALKING AROUND

For Pablo Neruda

It's possible that I don't realize
just how miserable I am.
I have left a life behind
that had meaning,
that defined me.
I have left behind my books,
my office, my gym,
I have left behind my life.

It's possible that I don't realize
just how miserable I am.
I walk about in a fog
like a poet grasping
for a metaphor,
like music searching
for a guitar,
or lips and teeth
and tongue crying out
for the music to come forth.

The broken wine glasses
of dawn make me fly
into the rage
of a homeless child.
Fox and CNN cough
and wretch like two drunks
beside an empty dumpster.

It's possible that I don't realize
just how miserable I am.
All I want is to lay down
in the slime and ooze
of the Euphrates,
to rest my head in the warm
mud of its estuary
and to take solace from
the flies buzzing overhead
where crabs eat the flesh
of the living and the dead.

Monday comes with the rage
of an eagle as it tears apart
the liver of a Prometheus
in the throes of social media.

All I want is the comfort
of the cross, to look down
upon the upturned faces,
bleeding and sweating
on those hoping for an answer
from one who is also
a searcher for an answer.

And yet I tell myself
that this morning
could be much worse.
I could be in a hospital
on a respirator

with a well-intentioned
nurse or other strangers
hovering over me.
My final agony an inconvenience,
of interest to no one present.

It's possible that I don't realize
just how miserable I am,
as the absolute solitude
of this life we call the new normal
slowly sinks in like bleeding tears
coagulating at sunset on an open wound
and brings back a time in our lives
when faith was the answer to Moloch.

2084

2084 is a true story about the end of the world:
the pump don't work cuz the vandals stole the handle

We are living in a world
known as IQ84
where 2020 vision
doesn't help us anymore.
We will never close the door
against the wind that's at our shores.
Tis the wind and nothing more...

Let me take you back in time
to a place where 1948 was 1984
for visionaries and the paranoid,
to a place where nothing was real
so we called it *Strawberry Fields.*

Thanks to Gates and thanks to Jobs
we are living inside a void,
this *Brave New World,*
spied upon by *Big Brother,*
this *Animal Farm,*
where all the pigs are equally ignored:
the millennium has come and gone,
and just like a thousand years before
we are the worker bees
with empty heads and empty dreams,
the hollow men, the men of straw,
living in a *Waste Land,* slaving away

at the master's beck and call.

In the Middle Ages the average man
could neither read nor could he write.
After the Renaissance, the Baroque,
Cervantes, Shakespeare, Milton and Pope,
After the Enlightenment & Romanticism
After Byron, Shelley, Voltaire and Diderot,
we have once again become our own joke.

After the Buda, Socrates, Plato, Christ and Mohammed.
After watching Rome, Greece, Europe, the Caliphates
come and go,
after knights in shining armor, gothic cathedrals,
after all our voyages of discovery, our science, our art,
our wars,
what does it mean to be human, dear soul?
Tell me, brave new soul, what do you live for in IQ84?
What would you die for beside that toy
that you clutch in your hand like the broadsword of old.

Will these questions make any sense in 2084?
Quoth the raven, *nevermore*.

WALT

Good morning, grand old man!
Some say, father of modern poetry,
but you sound old fashioned to me.
Not at all like hip hop, rap or rock 'n roll.
Who would have the patience to read you?
Consider Cervantes, who nobody reads.
We are like horses being led to the waters
of a wild and rambunctious river
with our bellies full of sweet grass and no thirst at all.
And yet the brilliance persists.
We feel obligated, Leaves of Grass, indeed.
A classic sleeping in the forests of oblivion.

A child asked what is the grass?
To which you replied you didn't know.
Maybe it was Dimitri's sticky green leaves of springtime,
or maybe it was the hair sprouting from a lover's chest,
or maybe it was the child itself, of hopeful green stuff
woven,
or maybe it was the beautiful uncut hair of graves. . .
To all of this we are but spectators,
riders of the storm that are not the storm.

You sprouted up out of the ground nourished
by the blood spilled in a civil war.
Your tender shoots appeared to push aside
the dead and desiccated leaves of a dying sun,

to show us the absolute chaos of a new and vibrant
world.
You first saw the runaway slave sitting by your woodpile:
you put plasters on the galls of his neck and his ankles,
you fed him and clothed him and shared your home
with him.
When he was able he continued on his journey of life.

You sing the song of ourselves:
you are our first Cosmic Connection.
You are our first carbon base copy of God.
You multiply our hopes and dreams
into the stardust that we share and are.

You scoff at human kind with its fear of God
and its arrogant civilizations,
with its pointless rules and regulations,
and you are all of us and we are you.
You are simple beyond simplicity,
the fundamental material of life.
You are the pure scope and magnitude
of all that dwells within us.

As my eyes fail and I still try to read
your words of grass
on the fading leaves of the page
that mocks my existence,
you praise all creatures
grand and in miniature,
from the humble titmouse
to the stallion that you sought to ride

in absolute freedom.
I promise to keep reading you, Walt,
and to keep learning from you,
with your lexicon on the verge of oblivion,
with your leaves of grass on the verge of extinction,
to be found, perhaps, on the sole of the traveler's shoe,
thou windy old man, thou hurricane of a poet.

THE ROAD

LONG before the Crackers cracked their whips
and the Seminoles faded into the palmettos
there were others who, almost upright,
migrated south down the spine of the peninsula.
And before them? The truth is nobody knows.
But they built this road with their bare feet
relentlessly as centuries gave way to millennia.

They grew in numbers, scratching a living
from the infertile sand,
enslaving the less fortunate,
exterminating the proud rattlesnake
and the hapless turtle
with their road and their machines.
Inventing poisons to kill everything:
Clordane, DDT, malathion, paraquat
All Green Must Perish, or so it seemed.

This house was once a forest
of pine and oak, of palmetto and sandspurs,
as humble as the grace of an Aztec god.
It was a stranger in a strange land,
a ship filled with sunrises and sunsets
with no compass or calendar to guide it.
When the abuelos arrived, they were as naked
as the Seminoles before them:
only the name Chapultepec remained.
They built this house beside the road,

far away from the lake with its flies and mosquitoes,
with its tiger that would one day feed on their souls.
They prospered, having survived a war in Mexico.
They enjoyed the Roaring Twenties, the Great Depression,
World War II, the Post War Boom, and then they died,
as most folks do.

Their seed was scattered far and wide,
no thought of them remained,
like those who had come before them,
like the coal miners from Wales
or San Luis Potosí with mescal plants
and spuds from their native lands.

Their sons and their daughters disappeared,
but the house remained, at anchor,
a restless ship, rocking us to sleep,
a candle in the wind, music by any other name.

Generations of people made pilgrimages
to *la casa de los abuelos*
along this road that began in Chapultepec Park
and ended where it began,
to sit on the porch of the house and to remember,
to lie on the beds with horsehair mattresses,
to die wrapped in its clean white sheets
(Compadre, quiero morirme…).

No one who was born here has ever left.
The dead live here in this orphanage of souls.
They look silently out of the windows at the road

as dawn rises up drenched in the blood of Wales.
They look out over the lake in the evening
as the sun sets somewhere in Mexico.

The snakes and turtles have long since gone.
The naked footprints in the sand
were followed by hard clay, gravel and crushed rock.
Monstrous vessels roll along its surface now.
No one dares walk on it any more.

In a singular act of defiance,
Artemisa's Oldsmobile is parked in the drive
with its 455 Rocket V8 ready to prowl,
with a bumper sticker that prays:
"If you must leave Florida please take a friend."
But still the road prevails, and now the Rat is king.

I remember sunsets as a boy, free from fear.

IN SEARCH OF RAMONET

Julio, silver and gold
won't buy back the life
of a heart grown cold
BOB DYLAN

I am Genaro Ramonet
the Yaquis murdered my father
and burned down our ranch in Sonora.
I fled for my life to San Luis Potosí
with my wife and two daughters
tangled up in blue.
My daughter Artemisa
married a gringo.
They had three children
before the Revolution struck
and they fled for their lives
across the border to California.

I am John Evans
born in Nantyglo, Wales,
I was forced to leave my home
when the coal mines closed down
in Nantyglo
only to wind up mining coal
in Pittsburgh.
My son John was too slight
and too smart to work in the mines.
He went to Mexico
and fell for a Mexican beauty.

They prospered, but then disaster
took its toll and they fled for their lives.

We are the Evans children
born of Ramonet.
Our seed has been scattered
throughout the North Country.
It has no future, no present, no past.
We are the children of war and famine,
but we hide it well: our hands are smooth
and our clothes are clean.
There is not a hint of Nahuatl
in the language that we speak.
But we have fallen prey to the memory plague
as we sit on the porch in *la casa de los abuelos*
and drink our iced tea pretending not to hear
the deep organ notes of the tiger
as it breathes in the twilight of the lake.

TENOCHTITLAN

Bob Dylan
looks into the darkness
and hears the song of a rattlesnake.
It is singing in the mouth of an eagle
flying above the desolation of Tenochtitlan.

There could be no greater satisfaction
than an Aztec death, he thinks,
heads
              bouncing down
                              the stones
of Teotihuacán, hearts beating
gently in the moonlight, your skin slowly
peeled off of you like lemonade in church.

Better than brain cancer like George,
or being shot full of holes like John,
you think as you make it down the aisle
to where your bride awaits you,
—the sad eyed lady tangled up in blue—
she who will not be denied.

HERE COMES THE SUN

For Richard Brautigan

Every morning
I wake up to these words
and the music of the dead
reaches out to me.
Yeah, you gotta enjoy
these moments
before they come to an end:
these sunrises,
as magnificent as they are,
once lit up the eyes
of John Lennon,
and those sunsets
that await you in the evening
caused the soul to vibrate
of Charles Baudelaire.

Every day we are diminished
in our own way.
If you are lucky, there will be
a moment in your day
that you will share with Buddy Holly.
If you are lucky, Mark Twain
will cast you a line
as his riverboat fades away.

I am old but fortunate:
as of yet, I have not heard

the unmistakable sound
of a single action Colt
inviting me to dream
in watermelon sugar
where the deeds will be done
once and forever,
and tigers sleep beneath the river
as moonlight plays on the banks
of the town of Ideath.

Richard, what was that moment like,
when everything inside of you was broken,
when the wine glasses of dawn
had not yet spoken to you,
when the first rays of dawn brought
Luis Buñuel's razor opening
the mind's eye in the mirror,
when the darkness settled about you
like Rimbaud's vision of hell
and you found yourself waiting alone
in that darkness for the words
of John, Paul, George and Ringo Starr.

SUMMER OF 64

I remember the women of Madrid
on their knees scrubbing
the sidewalks and stoops
in front of their doors with rags.

I remember the men of Madrid,
missing arms, missing legs, missing eyes,
limping along on wooden crutches
dressed in the rags
that the women washed every night.

JFK had been dead for the amount of time
It takes to make a baby
—*he not busy being born is busy dying*—
were words still unknown to you.

Camelot was a distant dream
blown up on a sunlit street in Dallas, Texas.
Something was happening,
but we didn't know what it was.

The blues and jazz were dying too
and as they faded into Shea Stadium
where the Beatles were playing
Norwegian Wood
you were plugging in at Monterrey
to lead us on our counter revolution.

The times they were a changing,
but we didn't know into what:
A Coney Island of the Mind, Howl,
Dharma Bums: we were all On the Road
to Viet Nam with Country Joe and the Fish.

THE DEATH OF SOCRATES
(A TRAGIC COMEDY IN THREE ACTS)

Jacques-Louis David
painted *The Death of Socrates* in 1787,
just two short years
before the French Revolution.
The nobility of the painting
belies the grim reality
of walking up the hillside
toward the three caves
with their rusty iron grates.
We were hot and sweaty,
with flies buzzing all around us
on that hot summer morning.
As he awaited execution by suicide
from the vantage point of his cell
he had a fine view of the government
that he had dared to question.

Francisco Goya
painted the Second of May 1808
to describe the slaughter
of the people of Madrid
at the hands of mercenaries,
Mamelukes, enlisted by Napoleon.
Later, his epic *Disasters of War*
chronicled the French invasion
of his country and the brave
resistance of the Spanish people.

The Sleep of Reason
led to Saturn Eating His Son,
and ended in his final madness,
in the paintings of witches,
violence, darkness and death.

Pablo Picasso
painted *Guernica* in June, 1937,
shortly after the Nazis
were invited, like the French
before them, to bomb
a humble village in the heartland
of the Basque region.
The painting is fragmented,
broken, distorted, insane.
No mercy was given:
hell rained down from above
like mustard gas, like agent orange,
like napalm, like the Atom bomb.
Hell rained down on helpless humanity.

He not busy being born is busy dying:
Plato, the old young man in the painting by David.

GRASSY KNOLL GRANADA

Please, don't murder me!
Your plea jumps right
out of that grass covered hole in Víznar,
along with the silenced cries of 2,000 other souls.

There is sun and there is wind,
wind that turns the leaves
of the poplar trees into machado
along the sierra.
                                    Yusef Komunyakaa
picks up a shotgun shell,
and then puts it back
exactly where he found it.
#8 birdshot.
                        They hunt up here, she says.

The bloodthirsty motherfuckers, I think.
If they can't kill each other they kill
anything that moves.

The afternoon suddenly turns cold
and he wind cries out for mercy
as you say to yourself,
it's not dark yet but it's getting there.

HAND ON A DEAD MAN'S STONE

We are still looking for you:
every year we come to this
inhospitable, ungodly place,
on a pitiful fragile pilgrimage
along a road that leads
from here back to your birth city.

Like the star you once were
you are buried everywhere,
yet invisible to all. We sit
beside the site of the mass grave,
walk down to the monument
by the pine trees, but always
return to the stone resting
in a bed of thorns between two olive trees.

I place my hand on this stone
warmed by your Andalusian sun
and feel a beating heart.

MEXICAN DEMO CRAZY

For Alí Calderón

In Alí Calderón's
Mexican Democracy
the Aztec gods of old
and the drug lords
of modern-day Mexico
come out at night
along with the rats,
mistresses of this land.

A newborn is found dead
and rotting in a plastic garbage
bag by the side of the road.
Severed heads roll about like
golf balls at the Augusta Nationals.
The Day of the Dead
has been every day in Mexico
for a very long time.

Uichilobos reminds us that
before the iron maiden or the rack,
before witches were burned at the stake,
before the guillotine, the garrote,
before mustard gas in the trenches,
before napalm in the jungles,
before the machine gun, land mines and IEDs,
before Colt, Browning, Kalashnikov or Stoner,
before death went full-automatic, lock 'n' load,

there was the *tecpatl*, a simple blade of flint or obsidian
that served its purpose well by ripping out
the still beating heart of the terrified victims.

In modern times the dead are not dignified with
a symbolic sacrifice on the top of Teotihuacan.
They are not murdered for any alleged purpose.
They are found everywhere, in the streets, in their cars,
in their offices, on their door stoops, in their beds.
They are reduced to their basic body parts:
eyes and ears and noses. Livers, pancreases, intestines.
Genitals, penises, finger nails, tongues and vocal chords.
Unlike in the case of Uichilobos, nobody knows who is who:
the guardias, the local police, the gangs, the politicians,
the kids on the street corners all look the same on the news.
It's all the same to the rats too: Mistresses of this land.

Octavio Paz got it right: *Viva México, hijos de la chingada!*

MANRIQUE

This is the Euphrates,
the Amazon, the Nile,
the Mississippi,
the cradle of then and now.

This is where life began
and begins anew every day,
and yours are the headwaters
that bring life to that child.

If only I could rest my head
in the mud and the slime
of the estuary of this great river,
this Mississippi
transfixed
by a harvest moon
filled with rose petals
and the dream of Botticelli.

Our lives are the rivers
that flow out into the sea
wrote the great Manrique
at the end of the 15th century.

As I lay down upon the bank
and listen to the water's song,
there is nothing here to understand:
just taste, touch, smile and move along.

GROUND ZERO

For Nieves in her Baeza

This is the room, the desk, the chair.
Instead of the warbling of students
your personal
and professional life on display:
your salary, your raise,
your briefcase on the wall,
your umbrella in the corner. . .

You were such a private soul
and here it is for all to see:
everything that doesn't matter.
There are no voices in the room
—*we are all silent*—
in awe that this still exists.
Outside there are poplar trees along the river
and dusty roads that once caused a traveler
to reflect and the reader to dream . . .

At 30,000 feet I feel closer to you now
and the *Soria fría* that you made me see.

A READING

Machado is resting on my lap
like no other lover ever has.
The fragile pages,
once crisp and cool to the touch
a century ago
are ready to crumble tonight
under the loving gaze and caress
of a faithful friend.

What happened to that dancing,
that soft music that they used to play?
a poet from the fifteenth century laments.

I want to take you to Baeza,
where he taught school, she says.
I nod my head but feel the darkness
settling in all around me.

The embers of a mauve twilight
spark a chill in my spine,
and I look down at the dust on my shoes
from a journey that surely awaits me.

As the master once said:
It's not dark yet, but it's getting there. . .
but still the pages maintain their integrity
for yet another reading,
and the words remain to comfort me.

ANTONIO

Era la buena voz
que escuchaba
¿Y qué tal tu familia?
Es que todos se han muerto
contestaba
Entonces, no hay manera
de consolarte
Sólo queda el llanto
y un momento profundo
para expresarlo
Cuando eso me decía
la buena voz
sentía un leve roce
en el hombro
Un angel a mi lado
dormitaba

THE ROSE AND THE HONEY BEES

en el silencia sólo se escuchaba
un susurro de abejas que sonaba.

*in the silence all that you could hear
was the whispering of the bees in your ears...*

GARCILASO DE LA VEGA

Walk down by the river,
reach out and touch
the rose bushes.
They are waiting for you,
but only one rose
will speak to you.
Your memories
are all you have:
treasure them along
with the whispering
of the honey bees,
the clouds, the sky
and what is left
before your eyes:
your heart, your mind.
Remember the sound
of the honey bees.

WAITING FOR BAUDELAIRE IN WALDEN

These morning trees don't remember you,
but there is something in the air you left behind,
something remains from last night.
These trees have borne witness to your presence:
you were here in the moonlight.
You traced a fragile journey through the sky,
like the smoke from a burning censor,
like the host offered to an outstretched hand,
like a mother's breast to a newborn child:
you were there by my side in my sleep.
I was waiting for you like a bride.

CONTENTS

CONTENTS